THE ACKERMANN MILITARY PRINTS
UNIFORMS OF THE BRITISH AND INDIAN ARMIES
1840-1855

THE ACKERMANN MILITARY PRINTS

UNIFORMS OF THE BRITISH AND INDIAN ARMIES
1840-1855

WILLIAM Y. CARMAN
WITH ROBERT W. KENNY, JR.

Schiffer Military History
Atglen, PA

Book design by Robert Biondi.

Copyright © 2003 by Willian Y. Carman.
Library of Congress Catalog Number: 2002112808.

Printed in China.
ISBN: 0-7643-1671-0

We are always looking for people to write books on new and related subjects. If you have an idea
for a book, please contact us at the address below.

Published by Schiffer Publishing Ltd.	In Europe, Schiffer books are distributed by:
4880 Lower Valley Road	Bushwood Books
Atglen, PA 19310	6 Marksbury Ave.
Phone: (610) 593-1777	Kew Gardens
FAX: (610) 593-2002	Surrey TW9 4JF
E-mail: Info@schifferbooks.com.	England
Visit our web site at: www.schifferbooks.com	Phone: 44 (0)208 392-8585
Please write for a free catalog.	FAX: 44 (0)208 392-9876
This book may be purchased from the publisher.	E-mail: Bushwd@aol.com.
Please include $3.95 postage.	Free postage in the UK. Europe: air mail at cost.
Try your bookstore first.	Try your bookstore first.

CONTENTS

INTRODUCTION

For many years the magnificent colour prints published by the firm of Rudolf Ackermann have been in the possession of lucky collectors. But with the passing of many years these frail works of art have become damaged, or have perished and failed to survive, so that many are not available to those who wish to find and appreciate the work and care which went into these productions.

To produce such prints required many processes, and much research was necessary. At first accurate information of the specialised uniform had to be found and confirmed with the rigid dress regulations of that time; it was also necessary to know the precise tailoring of the uniform and equipment. A competent artist would then have to produce a satisfactory drawing or water-colour of a typical soldier and perhaps a fully equipped horse. This result must then be transferred to a metal plate or stone by a capable engraver. A careful print had to be made on the correct paper and then colouring, often with qualified artists finalising with touches of gold or silver. This elaborate process, which would take much time and money, could not be repeated commercially these days, so one must be grateful that modern photogravure and illustration can produce an almost precise copy of the lost art.

As these desirable plates were once produced in saleable quantities it might be thought that today they could be easily found. For this volume, much time was spent searching the United Kingdom without complete success. The answer was finally found in the magnificent and priceless collection of the Anne S.K. Brown Military Collection at Brown University, Providence, Rhode Island, where prints in pristine condition were available. We are indebted to the generous assistance of the Curator of this collection, Peter Harrington, a well-known historical writer, and to the unstinting cooperation of Robert W. Kenny, that all the needed plates were selected and appear in this work.

• • •

The long-lived firm of Ackermann, under father and son, began at the end of the eighteenth century and produced prints during the reign of the Georgian kings, King William and Queen Victoria, before turning away from print making. Apart from the four portrait prints, the plates in this volume show the British uniform for several years plus a special group on the Armies of India. One may see how fame may have brought a regiment forward but it will be seen that cavalry prints were most popular, leaving many infantry regiments unnoticed. As it seems that no more than four prints were issued on one occasion, the advance in new plates was slow. Thus after a period of time uniforms went out of date and a new plate had to be made, or a previous plate altered to show the new items.

Although there were no continental wars for the British troops there were opportunities in the widely spread Empire, like the campaigns in South Africa, the constant tribal conflicts in the Indian peninsula and reasons for trouble in Canada. Normally Ackermann prints of uniforms show the Regular Army, and although the Cape Mounted Rifles might appear unusual, they were included in the Army Lists and did take part in the South African conflicts, 1834-1853, as did the British cavalry units. Being in India warfare seemed endless, with the First Afghan War from 1839-1843, the Scinde Campaign of 1843 followed by the Sikh Wars which included the Sutlej Campaign, December 1845 - February 1846 and the Punjabi Campaign, September 1848 - March 1849. Then the war that changed so much in the Army, the Crimean War, 1854-1856; but the effects of the Indian Mutiny, 1857-1858, were yet to come, although not recorded in these prints.

So this book brings together the work of a time which has not been well covered before, not only touching on history and the British Army, but allowing appreciation of these rare prints.

THE PLATES

Page 41
Queen Victoria
Her Majesty
Reviewing the First Grenadier Regiment Foot Guards

This large print, 11 inches by 9, was painted by Henry I. Daubrawa, engraved by John Harris and published on May 24, 1851. It was later republished by W. Tegg of London but without a date. It is difficult to state what date or occasion this review took place but as the Queen frequently was with her Foot Guards, it would not be needed. It will be noted that the Queen wears a semi-military dress, which seems to vary when she is depicted with her troops. On this occasion she has a very full riding habit, the skirts of which touch the ground. She also wears the Order and Star of the Garter. The horse furniture appears to be that of a field marshal as the elaborate saddle cloth has the devices of the Guelphic Crown: crossed batons and three stars. She is accompanied by mounted staff which includes a General Officer as her Aide-de-Camp and several officers of the Royal Horse Guards. As the Grenadier Guards make a salute, the regimental Colour is lowered to touch the ground.

Page 42
The Prince Consort
Field Marshal H.R.H. Prince Albert KG KT KP etc.
Colonel of the (Scots) Fusilier Guards
Artist: Henry I. Daubrawa • **Engraver**: John Harris
Published December 24, 1850

Albert, Duke of Saxony and Prince of Saxe-Coburg and Gotha, married Queen Victoria on February 10, 1820. He was made Field Marshal in the same month. In 1842 he became Colonel of the Scots Fusilier Guards (later Scots Guards) and when the Duke of Wellington died in 1852, he became Colonel of the Coldstream Guards as well as Colonel in Chief of the Rifle Brigade. He attended public duties but did not take part in any active campaign. This portrait shows him mounted in front of the Scottish Foot Guards; his uniform shows no plume in the bearskin but has buttons and gold loops in threes. The saddle cloth and holster caps are blue with much gold lace and embroidery; even today the Scots Guards have the same special state saddle cloth. The Prince's health was not good and he died in the winter of 1861.

Page 43
Major General H.R.H. the Duke of Cambridge K.G.
Commander of a Division of the Army in the East
Artist: Henry I. Daubrawa • **Engraver**: John Harris

At the outbreak of the Crimean War the Duke of Cambridge commanded the Guards Division, which first went to Malta, then proceeded to Bulgaria and finally to the Crimean peninsula. The Duke is accompanied by Staff Officers and an escort of the 17th Lancers, as they pass drummers of the Grenadier Guards. The Duke wears the uniform of a Major-General with the Sash and Star of the Order of the Garter. Later, as a Field Marshal, he was Commander-in-Chief of the British Army from 1856-1895. He was born in 1819 and died in 1904.

Page 44
The Duke of Wellington
Field Marshall His Grace the Duke of Wellington
K.G. G.C.B. G.C.H.
At the Grand Review in Windsor Great Park
Artist: Henry I. Daubrawa • **Engraver**: John Harris
Published June 18, 1845

The Duke of Wellington, though nominally head of the Army, was now more concerned with politics and not in the best of health. It is interesting to know that Queen Victoria held this Grand Review for the Emperor of Russia to review the Household Troops. Present were the Household Cavalry, all three regiments of Foot Guards and Royal Artillery from Woolwich. Within a few years the British nation was at war with Russia. The Duke wears a Field Marshal's uniform and the accompanying cavalry is the 17th Lancers. The Duke died on the September 15, 1852.

ACKERMANN LARGE PRINTS

On occasion, Rudolf Ackermann produced large plates, perhaps to show details more clearly or even to ask for a higher price. As the number of large plates was small, it may be that they were not quite the success expected. The size was approximately twenty by sixteen inches and there were only three large cavalry plates as shown here: 16th (Queen's) Lancers, 3rd (King's Own) Light Dragoons and 8th King's Own Royal Irish Light Dragoons. There were also four large portrait prints which appear earlier in the book: Queen Victoria, the Prince Consort, the Duke of Cambridge, and the Duke of Wellington.

Page 45
3rd (King's Own) Light Dragoons
Artist: Henry Martens • **Engraver**: John Harris
Published June 21, 1851

The first large cavalry plate was of the 16th Lancers and had been based on a distinguished Officer, Lieutenant-Colonel J.E. Smyth, but this large plate was not labeled as any particular person and no medal or decoration is shown as a clue, so it is assumed that no particular warrior is depicted. However the officers of the 3rd Light Dragoons had been engaged in so much recent warfare that any officer could have named himself as being portrayed, and be glad to own such a fine plate. The 3rd had been in the Sutlej Campaign: at Moodkee on 18 December, at Ferozeshaher three days later and then at Sobraon on 10th February 1846, when the Sikhs were totally defeated. A further rebellion broke out later in the same year which brought defeat to the natives at Chillianwallah (January 1849) and Goojerat (February 1849) thus bringing the Punjab to British India. The 3rd Light Dragoons had distinguished themselves in all these engagements but did not return home until 1853. The uniform is as expected for Light Dragoons but the regimental distinctions definitely make them the 3rd King's Own with the White Horse, dating back to ancient times, and the shabraque has the embroidered initials 'KOLD' indicating the regimental title.

Page 46
16th (Queen's) Lancers
Lt. Colonel J.R. Smyth, C.B. 1848
Artist: Henry Martens • **Engraver**: by John Harris
Published June 14, 1851

John Rowland Smyth, born in County Waterford, Ireland, was six feet tall and quite a character. He joined the 16th Lancers in 1821 but in 1831, when he was a captain, killed an opponent in a duel. He was sentenced to twelve months' imprisonment but was granted one year's leave. In 1839 he served with the 6th Dragoons but returned to the 16th Lancers in 1842. The Regiment was still stationed in the Punjab in India where it had been for many years, when in 1845, the Sikh Army crossed the Sutlej and the British Army had to take action. Major Smyth was in command of the 16th

Queen's Lancers at the battle of Aliwal in 1846, where they lost fifty-eight men killed and sixty-five wounded, thus losing one third of their strength. After this action he was made a Lieutenant-Colonel and awarded the C.B., eventually becoming a Lieutenant-General. The uniform is similar to that in 'SMALL' No.3 (1844) , with no special differences to be noted. His plumed lance-cap indicates that he was not portrayed during military action as his men wore cased lance-caps in combat.

Page 47
8th King's Own Royal Irish Light Dragoons
Artist: Henry Martens • **Engraver**: John Harris
Published May 18, 1852

Although the wording on this plate does not mention Hussars, this is an oversight as the regiment portrayed here had been converted to Hussars in 1822. They served at home in the 'long peace' and nowhere abroad. But two years after this plate was made they were in the Crimean War. Their uniform had been depicted in 1844, as Plate No.25 of *Costume*, which showed a similar officer but from the right side. However this plate does show well the full dress sabretache: red cloth face with much embroidery, the five-hooped Crown over a 'V R' cypher which had the Royal Crest on it. Below was 'VIII' over the female Harp flanked by a scroll with 'THE KING'S ROYAL' on one side and on the other a scroll with 'IRISH HUSSARS.' The corners were filled with shamrocks and the lace all round was of shamrock pattern. The blue shabraque repeated some of this, the 'VR' cypher, the Royal Crest over the Harp and below 'VIII' over 'H.'

Page 48
British Cavalry
2nd Life Guards (Officer)
Published September 1, 1840

This plate has the earliest date in the *Costumes of the British Army* series but was not given a number. But the plate has much text to give information. Immediately below the plate, small lettering states: 'W. Henry I. Daubrawa pinxt. On Stone by A.O. Driscoll.' On the far right is: 'Day and Haghe lith' (who no doubt helped in the production). But at the bottom of the plate, to remove all doubt as to the publisher is: 'London. Published by R. Ackermann Eclipse Sporting Gallery 191 Regent Street. Sept. 1st 1840'. This plate remained in production until it was replaced by a second state in January 1844 which was numbered '1'. The uniform depicted is an unusual one for the Household Cavalry, who normally wore a hat or helmet. But there was a precedent for fur caps when the Horse Grenadier Guards existed up to 1788. Perhaps it was the award of fur caps to the Foot Guards that led to the restoration of the Household Cavalry's fur caps which were worn from 1820-1842. The 2nd Life Guards tended to emphasise their connection with grenadiers and wore a grenade over the '2' on the horse furniture and elsewhere. Notice that the troopers carry a musket or firearm instead of a sword to confirm this aspect.

Page 49

British Cavalry

2nd Life Guards

Artist: Henry Martens • **Engraver:** J.W. Giles

Published January 1, 1844

New Appointments

This plate was actually numbered '1' but as seen by the date came out much later than the original plate. The first plate was re-engraved to produce the new appointments by changing the bearskin to the new helmet; also altered were the saddle-cloth and the background figures. The group on the left was reduced to a side view of a state trumpeter and the troopers were now given swords instead of firearms. The new helmet of German silver had been introduced in 1842 to the Household Cavalry. The saddle-cloth was now fully rounded at the rear and on it the grenade of the old pattern is replaced by the Royal Crest over the silver Garter Star. Battle honours were on each side of the star and below all was the number '2'. The Life Guards were to be seen performing duties in London but were not in any section at this time.

Page 50

Royal Artillery

Artist: W. Heath • **Engraver:** A.O. Driscoll

Published October 8, 1840

When first issued this plate did not carry a number. Later for a time it was numbered '1' but when the series became larger and was reorganised, it was finally numbered '2.' This plate shows the Foot-Artillery in marching order firing a 3 or 6 pounder field piece. In the sky above may be seen the flame of a rocket. The dress of the Royal Artillery shows the broad-topped shako of 1839 which was changed in 1846 to the straight-sided cylinder pattern. The gunners wear blue coats with red facings and yellow lace, whereas the officers have gold lace and embroidery. The men's buttons are brass while those of the officers are gilt. The gunner in front carries a long rod on which is a sponge for damping down the hot barrel of the gun; it also acted as a rammer for packing gun-powder, shot and wads down the barrel ready for firing. The commanding officer is mounted, as is his 'signaler', the trumpeter in the red coat who sounds the officer's orders. The 'reversed' colours of the coat were worn until the Crimean War and then finally discontinued.

Page 51

Rifle Brigade

(The Brigade in Battle)

Artist: W. Heath • **Engraver:** A.O. Driscoll

Published January 1, 1841

The Rifle Brigade officer is wearing a wide-topped shako, then called a black beaver cap, on the front of which was a bronze (blackened) plate and a black silk ball tuft. Under the chin was a bronzed metal chin-chain. The dress jacket was rifle green with black collar and pointed cuffs. The trousers were also rifle green with side stripes of

black mohair braid. The shoulder belt of black leather had silver fittings carrying many battle honours as well as a whistle and chain. The black waist belt has silver mountings and the traditional snake-clasp. The gloves were black leather. The dead cuirassier is an imaginary European enemy, not necessarily French but given red overalls and a 'modern' uniform coat of the Napoleonic period. The Rifle Brigade was fighting in South Africa in 1846-1847 and 1850-1853.

Page 52

Trumpeter, Royal Horse Guards Blue

Artist: W. Heath • **Engraver:** A.O. Driscoll

Published May 15, 1841

Although named as a trumpeter, the figure on the horse is a mounted kettle drummer. The back view of the trumpeter shows a slung trumpet, on the crimson banner of which the Royal Arms are embroidered. The kettle drum banner is elaborately embroidered with another version of the Royal Arms. Both men wear the State uniform which is not regimental, as the gold laced garments came from the Sovereign. This traditional dress dates back to Charles II and continues in use to the present day, varying only by the cypher of the Sovereign, worn on back and front. In the background may be seen a trooper of the Blue wearing the bearskin cap, soon to become obsolete.

Page 53

Royal Horse Guards, Blue

Artist: W. Heath • **Engraver:** A.O. Driscoll

Published May 15, 1841

The coat of the Blues is the reverse colouring of the Life Guards, being blue with red facings, instead of red with blue facings; they were only accepted as Household Cavalry in 1819. The first print of this series showed the Life Guards with fur caps; here the Blues have red plumes going across the tops instead of the white of the Life Guards. Worn as early as 1833, the fur cap was used in its last days in the Household Cavalry. The officer wears a waist sash of crimson and gold threads with the heavy pendant tassels flying out behind. The deep red saddle-cloth is pointed at the rear, with gold lace going all around, enclosing the embroidered Crown over an eight-pointed silver star.

Page 54

Royal Horse Guards, Blue

Windsor Castle

Full Dress, Parade Dress & Undress

Artist: W. Heath • **Engraver:** J.W. Giles

Published May 16, 1841

Although this plate is dated one day after the previous plate (also depicting the RHG Blues), there is a change in the fur cap: as its design becomes simpler it no longer has the gilt grenade or the tassels. The two guards are now clearly shown with the red flask-cord on the pouch-belt and whereas the officer has fringed epaulettes, these troopers have shoulder scales only. White leather pantaloons were worn for 'dress' occasions but for 'Leveas and Drawing Rooms' dark blue trousers with gold side-stripes were worn. For undress, officers wore red stripes like the men. The back view of a trooper in undress shows the wide red band on the blue undress cap and the waist-strap for the sword. A back view of a trumpeter in State dress shows the Crown over 'V.R.' on his back.

Page 55
Royal Horse Guards, Blue
(2nd State)
Published January 1, 1844

This plate is the one published on May 16, 1841, but with the new date and with bearskins deleted and replaced by silver helmets and red hair plumes. All else remains the same as first published.

Page 56
42nd Highlanders
Artist: W. Heath • **Engraver:** J.W. Giles
Published August 2, 1841

Although the artist depicts the men of the Black Watch in strict uniform, he shows a light touch with a dog chasing a duck and the hefty Scots crowding across a narrow bridge, with the regimental colours furled and covered, and with the mounted commanding officer looming up in the middle. The flying feather bonnet with the red hackle is now definitely the Black Watch's own distinction. The coatee is scarlet with blue facings and gold lace for the officers. Here the officer has epaulettes but the men have the white tufted wings of a flank company. The full tartan of the kilt shows material at the rear to indicate a shoulder plaid attachment. The white sporran for the officers would have gold tassels but those for the men should be black. The low black shoes with elegant gilt or brass buckles seem inadequate for serious marching.

Page 57
2nd Royal North British Dragoons
Artist: W. Heath • **Engraver:** J.W. Giles
Published August 15, 1841

Once again the artist depicts an attack on an unknown soldier which allows the officer of the better-known Scots Greys to make a spirited counter-attack (although the regiment had not been engaged in any recent battles). The bearskin cap appears to have a gilt grenade in front and tassels on the right side which may be the last use of these ornaments, as a picture circa 1842 shows a plain fur cap. The tall white feather plume goes across the top of the cap (as do the red plumes of today's musicians) but the 1846 Dress Regulations state the white hackle feather should be nine inches long and be worn upright. In the background may be seen an officer wearing a cocked hat with an upright white plume, possibly a quartermaster, not often seen in a cavalry charge. All the men are mounted on the 'greys' which normally appear as white, and which had been the special horse of this regiment for many years.

Page 58
4th Royal Irish Dragoon Guards
Field Officer of the Day
Artist: Henry I. Daubrawa • **Engraver:** J.W. Giles
Published November 1841

The 4th Dragoon Guard Officers wore a scarlet coat with blue velvet facings and nine gilt uniform buttons down the front. The collar and cuffs had pairs of gold lace loops. A gilt-brass helmet had been worn from 1843-1847, which could have had a crest with either a lion head or a long black mane with a black tuft in front. In 1847 these gave way to the Germanic 'Albert' helmet with a hair plume hanging from a central spike. Unfortunately the helmet in de Daubrawa's drawing is like neither. It is said that the second state of the plate has the later helmet with a spike but this is not available and so a date cannot be quoted. The dark blue overalls have gold side stripes. The horse furniture has black fur holster covers and a square cut saddle cloth of dark blue with gold lace and embroidery but no throat plume for the horse.

Page 59
The Royal Horse Artillery
Artist: Henry I. Daubrawa • **Engraver:** J.W. Giles
Published January 1, 1842

Horse artillery was formed to accompany cavalry formations and to be in action as soon as possible. So on their creation they assumed light cavalry dress with a helmet but in later Georgian times took the hussar busby or fur cap. At this time the officers' dark blue jacket was covered with gold cords and lace but not obscuring the scarlet collar and cuffs. The mounted gunners wore a similar dress but the gold was replaced with yellow braid and cord. The officers' broad black fur cap had a hanging red bag and the large feather plume in a gilt holder was plain white to indicate artillery. At this period the gun and limber is shown drawn by gunner drivers with men of the gun team mounted on the limbers ready to dismount and fire the gun. Later the gun team was mounted on their own horses, but closely accompanied the limbered gun. It will be noticed that their full dress varies little from the King's Troop of the Royal Artillery of today.

Page 60
11th (or Prince Albert's Own) Hussars
Artist: Henry I. Daubrawa • **Engraver:** J.W. Giles
Published January 1, 1842

The 11th Light Dragoons were converted into Hussars in 1840 and were named Prince Albert's Own Hussars when the Prince Consort became the colonel. With so high-ranking a colonel, a new and very distinctive uniform was created, using crimson for the facings and the dress overalls. Although the expensive fur busby with a crimson plume was worn on special occasions, on others plain shakos were worn. When he left the Regiment in 1842, the Prince Consort requested that no changes should be made in the name or the uniform without official sanction. The flying pelisse may appear to be ornamental, but in cold weather it became the outer garment as cloaks were only permitted later. Although the Regiment was not in action at this time they are shown attacking 'French-like' cavalrymen to add glamour. There was a fine mounted band of musicians which further distinguished itself by wearing a white or cream-coloured fur busby which had additional crimson ornaments such as the plume, the bag and the cords.

Page 61
Officer of the 15th (King's) Hussars
Artist: Henry I. Daubrawa • **Engraver:** J.W. Giles
Published March 15, 1842

Although permitted a fur busby, this officer wears a broad-topped red shako which was soon to change to a straight sided red pattern. The red shako had been worn when the regiment was fighting Napoleon, so the Dress Regulations made a special note that the 15th Hussars had 'permission to wear a scarlet cloth shako according to regimental pattern'. There was an intention for all regiments of hussars to wear a common basic uniform, differing only by badges and regimental distinctions. Thus for a period they all wore a dark blue jacket with dark blue collar and cuffs. The pelisse was also to be all blue and of course since 1830 all lace and embroidery was gold. All were to have the fur busby with a red bag plus the basic plume of the period. But as undress caps were worn, the 15th managed to claim a red shako for themselves. The full dress horse cloth of hussars was a shabraque with long pointed rear ends. The colour was scarlet for the 10th and 15th Hussars (other hussars having a different colour) for undress; a stout cover of leopardskin or spotted tigerskin could be worn by different regiments.

Page 62
12th Royal Lancers
Artist: Henry I. Daubrawa • **Engraver:** John Harris
Published April 20, 1849

In William IV's reign, Lancers had worn red jackets, and the 12th had blue facings – a colour given to the tops of their lance caps. In 1849 the red coat was obsolete and blue coats were worn, the red now becoming the regimental facing. It might be expected that the top of the lance-cap should change to red but the artist shows the old colour. However the 1846 Dress Regulations stated that the top of the lance-cap should be the colour of the facings, i.e. red, which continued to modern times. The lancer's jacket had two parallel rows of buttons on the front (not the plastron front) and red piping down the sleeves and on the back. Not shown in the plate is the gold bullion fringe worn on the middle of the back. Hanging from

the waist-belt is a sabretache, the front of which has the embroidered device of the 12th (Prince of Wales Royal) Lancers, of a Crown over 'VR' with 'XIII' below, all set on crossed lances, and based on a sabretache of King George IVth's time.

Page 63
1st Life Guards
Artist: Henry I. Daubrawa • **Engraver:** John Harris
Published May 15, 1842

The 2nd Life Guards had already been presented as a plate but since Household Cavalry was always a popular subject the 1st Life Guards now had their own plate, although there is not much difference to be seen. However each regiment was known to have its own distinctions. Household Cavalry wore helmets of German silver with white hair plumes for the Life Guards; There were minor differences in the fittings although the front plate of St. George's Star was in common use. The flask-cord for the 1st Life Guards was red although not clearly shown in this print. The dark blue saddle cloth was angular in shape and not with rounded ends as in the 2nd. The broad gold lace all around had blue edges on the outside. The embroidered devices were the Crown cypher of reversed 'VR' and an eight pointed silver star with the red Cross of St. George in a blue Garter.

Page 64
IXth (or Queen's Royal) Lancers
Artist: Henry I. Daubrawa • **Engraver:** John Harris
Published August 20, 1842

The 9th Lancers had arrived in India in 1842. At this time they were not yet engaged in action although in a couple of years they would be gaining battle honours. Lancers had been wearing red jackets in the reign of William IV but in 1840 these garments were again made in blue cloth. Thus the regimental facings which had been blue on a red coat now changed to scarlet according to a War Office Order. The overalls which had once been light blue were now dark blue. The gold lace down the officers' trousers had a pattern called 'clouded bias.' The 9th Lancers were permitted to wear a special type of lance cap. The large front plate had two oval shields: the Royal Arms and those of Queen Adelaide, whose cypher was also carried because she was the Queen referred to in their title. Instead of a coloured cloth top, they had black patent leather and instead of the gold lace of earlier days, they had a gilt-brass band around the middle, as shown in the plate.

Page 65
The Royal Horse Guards
Artist: Henry I. Daubrawa • **Engraver:** John Harris
Published January 2, 1843

The Royal Horse Guards Blues had appeared earlier in the *Costumes of the British Army* series (Plates 4, 5 and 6) but the introduction of a new helmet to the Household Cavalry regiments was a good reason for a new plate. As had been noted earlier the regiments of the Household Cavalry had worn a similar uniform but with varying colours and special minor differences. The new pattern helmet had just been introduced and was worn by all three regiments. It was the hair plume of red that distinguished the Royal Horse Guards from the white of the two Life Guards. It will be noted that the officer in the plate has a widespread aspect to the plume, much different from that of today; but this may be only the artistic treatment by the painter, who also made the large gold epaulettes and the stout aiguillette into magnificent features. White breeches and high black boots were normal features of the Household Cavalry but the horse furniture varied. The Blues officer has a scarlet horse cloth or shabraque with a border of two rows of gold lace and a line of blue cloth in between. The fronts were rounded and the deep pointed rears were embroidered with the Crown and Garter Star. An opportunity was taken to make Plate 6 into this second state by altering the fur caps to the new helmet, the remainder of the uniform needing no change.

Page 66
Officer of the 7th (Queen's Own) Hussars
Artist: Henry Martens • **Engraver**: John Harris
Published May 15, 1843

The 7th or Queen's Own Hussars had been serving in Canada for many years but returned to England in November 1842. The uniform shown in this plate had been authorised for many years. The broad-topped shako dated back to Georgian times but in Canada the head-dress varied in the local conditions due to very cold weather. However in the plate it is shown as 'full dress' with the top gold lace and braid. The officers' plume was of black cock-tail feathers and the men had black hair plumes (as did the officers for undress). The fastened pelisse is shown as a cold weather garment; in William IV's reign it had been scarlet but was officially changed back to blue in 1840. Although it is shown in blue here, it has been stated that the 7th did not change until 1844. The jacket worn below the pelisse and the overalls were also of dark blue cloth. In contrast to the dark uniform the sabretache had a scarlet cloth face with distinctive embroidery. William IV's Queen was Adelaide and although many 'Queen's' regiments used the cypher 'A.R.' the 7th Hussars did not, but in keeping with their 'Queen's Own' title, used the monogram of 'Q.O.', a practice which they continued to modern times.

Page 67
Officer of the Queen's Own Hussars
Artist: Henry Martens • **Engraver**: John Harris
Published May 15, 1843 (same date as No.17)

Once again a change in the uniforms brought a new plate for the 7th Queen's Own Hussars; this was the introduction of a new head-dress, the busby. So it was Plate 17 that was given a second state and used for the change of the shako to the busby. There was no change of any other item, not even the date. The restored busby had the red bag and the white over red plume as worn at Waterloo by hussars. The sabretache and the shabraque continued to be worn. The shabraque was said to have been inspired by that worn by the Prussian Hussars, being dark blue with scarlet vandykes within the gold lace border. Little more may be said as the two plates are so similar.

Page 68
XIIIth Light Dragoons
Artist: Henry I. Daubrawa • **Engraver**: John Harris
Published December 12, 1844

The Light Dragoons had returned to the original blue jacket when the red garment of William IV went out of use c.1842. Whereas it might seem that the Lancers had similar garments to those worn by the Light Dragoons, the Lancers had a single row of gilt buttons down the front and a plain back. Collars and cuffs were in the colour of the Regiment, facings white, in this case actually buff. Light Dragoons had pointed cuffs with gold embroidery, then changed to scarlet and gold. The broad-topped shako was still in wear and the large gilt Maltese cross plate in front was worn by the Eleventh Light Dragoon Regiment with a white feather plume. The horse cloth was of the normal dark blue, rounded, with regimental lace and regimental devices. As Light Dragoons had originally been infantry men they still carried a firearm, a carbine being their principal weapon.

Page 69
6th Dragoon Guards (Carabiniers) Officer
Artist: Henry I. Daubrawa • **Engraver**: John Harris
Published January 12, 1844

This regiment began life in 1685 as the Queen Dowager's Regiment of Horse but was known in 1692 as the King's Carabiniers because instead of swords their main weapon was a carbine, a short firearm not normally carried by cavalrymen. In 1788 they became known as the 6th Dragoon Guards (Carabiniers). Although the red coatee of the William IV period had been changed back to blue, the Dragoon Guards and Dragoons continued in their traditional scarlet coat. The gilt-brass helmet with a high black hair mane had been introduced in 1843. The scarlet jacket may have looked similar for the Dragoon Guards and the Dragoons but instead here the cuff is obscured by the white gauntlet gloves. The sabretache has a white face. The horse cloth for the Dragoon Guards was of a simple rectangular shape, carrying the embroidered device of a crown over 'VR' and silver crossed carbines in a gold sprig of laurel.

Page 70
Xth (The Prince of Wales' Own) Royal Regt of Lt Dragoons
Artist: Henry I. Daubrawa • **Engraver**: John Harris
Published February 1, 1844

As all hussar regiments had been derived from the Light Dragoons, the compilers of the Army Lists continued to call them Light Dragoons, only occasionally making enlightenment by mentioning in brackets 'Hussars' or 'Lancers.' The dress now shown is very similar to that introduced in 1814 for all hussars, which endeavoured to give them a single identifying costume; but there were many reasons for making differences. Here is clearly shown the old pattern of busby: tall with a narrow red bag on the right, cords around the crown, and now with the addition of a black chin-strap. White over red was the accepted plume for this regiment. There can be no doubt as to the regiment of the wearer of the scarlet sabretache as it has a very prominent gilt 'X' (the Roman numeral for ten) and the Prince of Wales' Feathers behind the gold crown, which show who was the earlier commander. Later known as the 10th Royal Hussars (Prince of Wales' Own), in 1969 the Regiment became the Royal Hussars (Prince of Wales' Own).

Page 71
49th (The Princess Charlotte of Wales') Regiment of Foot
Officers of the Flank Companies
Artist: Henry Martens • **Engraver:** John Harris
Published February 10, 1844

This regiment was raised in 1743, became the Herefordshire Regiment in 1782 and then in 1816 had the additional honour to be the 'Princess Charlotte of Wales' Regiment.' The regimental facings on the collar and cuffs were dark green, as was the horse cloth. The two officers wear the uniform common to most infantry at that time. The straight-sided Albert shako was introduced in 1844. In this version of the shako, the Battalion company officer's shako ball-tuft was white and red, the Grenadier companies' were all white and the Light Infantry companies' were green. The red ball shown here is unusual for the 49th. Although later Royal Regiments were allowed to have red, the 49th were not Royal until 1885. Both officers wear flank company wings instead of epaulettes, the one on the right being Light Infantry and the one on the left being Grenadier company. The long tailed coatee had been introduced in 1838 and was worn until 1855. For undress, officers wore a blue frock coat and cap, the latter with regimental lace in front. In 1881 their title was changed to the Berkshire Regiment.

Page 72
XVIIth Light Dragoons (Lancers)
Artist: Henry I. Daubrawa • **Engraver:** John Harris
Published June 1, 1844

Lancers who had been wearing a red jacket changed to blue in 1840. The 17th Lancers retained their white facings for the collar, cuffs and welts on the sleeves and back. The upper part of the lance cap was also of white cloth and the plume was of black cock-tail feathers for the officers and black hair for the men. The front plate obvi-ously carried the badge of the skull and 'OR GLORY,' as worn in their earliest days. Down the front of the blue jacket. were two rows of gilt buttons. The epaulettes and belts were made of gold wire but the top of the pouch was silver plate. White gauntlet gloves were worn by lancer officers. In the background may be seen the mounted band wearing the lancer uniform similar to the men's but distinguished by the red horsehair plumes on the lance caps. Stationed at home and seeing little trouble in Ireland, the 17th Lancers were due to see active service in the Crimean War in a few years' time.

Page 73
The 2nd or Coldstream Guards
Artist: Henry Martens • **Engraver:** John Harris
Published August 20, 1844

The Foot Guards were always a popular subject with the public and although these regiments may appear similar at first, each regiment was proud of its own distinctions which can be recognised. Although the Coldstream Guards were allocated a second place (the First Foot Guards had been formed by Charles II, the Second Foot Guards came from General Monk's troops already existing in England), they claimed that they were Nulli Secundus ('Second to None') and did not use the word 'second' although they did have their buttons in pairs. There are other differences. The Dress Regulations for Officers state that, 'the Coldstream Guards has the Star of the Order of the Garter on the collar, that the buttons are placed two and two, bars of embroidery and the skirt and flap also two and two. On the gold epaulettes Field Officers have the Crown, Garter Star and the Rose; the Captains and Subalterns the Rose only. In their bearskin caps the Coldstream Regiment has a scarlet feather ten inches long worn on the right side.'

Page 74
Ensign of The 1st or Grenadier Guards
Artist: Henry Martens • **Engraver:** John Harris
Published September 9, 1844

For their military success against Napoleon's Old Guard at Waterloo, the 1st Foot Guards were named Grenadier Guards in 1816 and thus gained special permission to wear the bearskin caps of grenadiers, who were always the foremost fighters in an infantry regiment. The Grenadier Guards wore a seven inch plume of white goat's hair on the left side of the fur cap, a position which an inspecting officer would recognise. They also had a silver grenade on each end of the collar, while buttons and loops were set at equal distances (called regular or one by one). Officers' epaulettes carried silver grenades, captains had a crown above the grenade and field officers, a crown and the Royal cypher as well. Ensigns were the lowest rank of officer and traditionally they carried the Ensign or regimental colour. Although the colour belt went across the left shoulder, the sword-belt went across the left.

Page 75
**VIIIth (The King's Royal Irish) Light Dragoons
Hussar Officer**
Artist: Henry I. Daubrawa • **Engraver**: John Harris
Published November 7, 1844

The 8th (King's Royal Irish) Light Dragoons had been converted into Hussars in 1824 to replace the 18th Hussars, who had been disbanded a few years earlier. The hussar dress to which they changed unfortunately lacked the fur cap, and the broad-topped shako was worn. Luckily the fur cap was restored to Hussars in 1842 and so this plate notes its reappearance. It will be seen in the print that the busby at that time was taller and thinner than the fur busby of today. The bag is red and the plume white over red as was common for hussars at that early time. The all blue jacket of officers had gold lace and braid with five rows of gilt buttons. The dark blue pelisse is fur lined and hangs on the left. The dark blue overalls shown here have gold lace side stripes. The pouch belt was covered with gold lace and had a pouch with scarlet facings. The crimson and gold girdle was standard wear for Hussar officers. The horse furniture includes a leopardskin edged with red cloth, as well as a blue shabraque carrying gold embroidered devices such as the 'VR' and a Crown over a gold Harp within silver sprays of shamrock, while below all this is a gold 'VII' and 'H.' Although not in combat at the moment, these Irish Hussars were due to fight several battles in the Crimean War.

Page 76
**The 3rd or Scots Fusilier Guards
Light Infantry Skirmishing**
Artist: Henry Martens • **Engraver**: John Harris
Published March 20, 1846

At last the 3rd Regiment of Foot Guards appears with the unusual title of Scots Fusilier Guards. Actually the Coldstream Guards were also to be known as Fusiliers but they refused to alter their name. Eventually in 1877 the Scots were allowed to drop the term 'Fusiliers.' They were expected to wear a white plume but they insisted that their fur caps needed no mark since when on parade they were in the middle. The basic coatee for foot guards had buttons in threes and their collar badge was the thistle. On the officers' epaulettes was the badge of the Thistle plus a Crown for Captain, and Crown and St. Andrew's Cross for Field Officers. White trousers were still being worn at home in the summer season: 1st May to 14th October. For the rest of the year trousers of Oxford mixture (a dark grey) were worn.

Page 77
**21st Royal North British Fusiliers
Officers in Full and Undress**
Artist: Henry Martens from a sketch by
Capt. Fred. Ainslie 21st Fusiliers • **Engraver**: John Harris
Published February 26, 1846

These Fusiliers had been named 'North British' when in 1712 the Scots Army entered the English establishment, and they retained that odd title until 1877 when they became the Royal Scots Fusiliers. Captain Ainslie, who supplied Messrs Ackermann with this information, also received mention when he gave much help for the 'Armies of India' plates (see below). The tall bearskin hat shown here without a white plume had been replaced in the 1846 Dress Regulations by a black beaver shako with a white worsted ball-tuft and a grenade plate, so the bear-skin in the plate was obsolete, but in India where the new headdress had not arrived, the bearskin was being worn out. When an infantry regiment was equipped with 'fusils' (a type of firearm), they were named fusiliers, an original title which they maintained even when others were similarly equipped. The badge of a grenade was worn on the belt-plate, the wings and elsewhere.

Page 78
The 4th (The Queen's Own) Light Dragoons
Artist: Henry Martens • **Engraver**: John Harris
Published April 11, 1845

The Regiment had been so named in 1818 but in 1861 became the 4th Queen's Own Hussars. From an era when all light regiments were light dragoons there had been many conversions. At this time there were only four remaining and all these were changed in 1861 to hussars. The headdress was a shako, or chaco as it was called at that date, made of black beaver, the front of which had a large Maltese Cross plate with regimental distinctions. The plumes were white feather for officers and hair for the men. The dark blue jacket had red facings for all regiments (except the 13th who had buff) and down the front a double row of gilt or brass buttons. The blue overalls had double stripes down each side. On the right in the picture is a trumpeter or bugler. He wears a distinctive red hair plume to denote a musician and instead of the usual blue shabraque, he has a brilliant scarlet version with yellow lace. The regiment had been in action in Afghanistan, Ghuznee in 1840, but its next battles were to be in the Crimea.

Page 79
XVIth (The Queen's) L.D. Lancers
Artist: Henry I. Daubrawa • **Engraver**: John Harris
Published June 24, 1845

The 16th Light Dragoons had been converted to lancers in 1816 and went on overseas service to India in 1832. There they wore the red jackets favoured by William IV who wished to retain blue for the Royal Navy. The 16th Lancers were involved in the battles of Ghuznee in 1840 and Maharajpore in 1844. When most of the light cavalry changed back into blue jackets in 1840 the 16th Lancers did not but continued to wear red or scarlet, a distinction which they maintained with pride into modern times. As the facings were blue, fitting for a Royal regiment, this was the colour for their collars and cuffs, as well as the welts on their jackets. The scarlet slashed flaps on each cuff had five small buttons and, instead of the bullion back pieces worn by lancers, the 16th had two buttons in the middle of the back and slashed flaps on the skirts with three regimental buttons on each. The top of the lance cap was dark blue cloth and the officers' plumes were black cock's feathers.

Page 80

The 6th (Inniskilling) Dragoons
Artist: Henry I. Daubrawa • **Engraver**: John Harris
Published July 28, 1845

The Inniskilling Dragoons were an ancient regiment from the old Irish Army and occasionally, with English and Scottish men, formed part of a Union Brigade. The gallant officer is wearing the gilt helmet which was introduced in 1844 and worn until 1849. The flowing black hair plume was worn by both officers and horses but white horsehair was for the band and, it is said, red for the trumpeter. Heavy cavalry wore a single-breasted scarlet coat with nine gilt buttons down the front. Gold loops were worn on the sleeves, three at equal distances for the heavy dragoons while the Dragoon Guards had four, a distinction usually hidden by the long gauntlet gloves. Saddle cloths were in the usual dark blue with square corners but distinguished by the single row of gold lace (two for Dragoon Guards) and the embroidered device of the impressive Castle of Enniskillin (Inniskilling) for the officers. Black sheepskins were also worn. In 1922 the 6th Dragoons were linked with the 5th Dragoon Guards and became known as the 5th Royal Inniskilling Dragoon Guards.

Page 81

6th Inniskilling Dragoons
Artist: Henry I. Daubrawa • **Engraver**: John Harris
Published July 28, 1845

To reflect a change in the uniform this plate was based on that of the same date 1845 but has altered heads to show the new helmet of 1849. This was known as an Albert helmet and had a black hair plume. The dress shabraque is also removed. The rest of the uniform is as described in No.30. An unusual feature is the single medal and ribbon on the chest. In the first state the ribbon is shown as blue/red/blue and in the second state as blue/white or pink/blue. Blue/red/blue was used for several decorations but the problem is finding which applies to the Inniskilling Dragoons. The Waterloo Medal was worn by many of the 6th Dragoons but the last in service was Quarter Master Frederick McDowell who was still in the regiment in 1843. The regiment then served in home stations until the Crimean War and thus had no campaign medals till then. It is possible that an officer had served in another regiment and gained a Military General Service Medal but none is known to have done. The fact that the medal ribbon in the second state is uncertain may indicate that the medal was a glorifying addition without specific identification.

Page 82

Royal Engineers
Artist: Henry Martens • **Engraver**: John Harris
Published May 20, 1846

Royal Engineers were part of the Board of Ordnance and all officers were specialists in their particular professions. At this time they could call upon the Sappers and Miners or even an infantry body to undertake the manual work. As they were not considered combatant, they did not wear a 'fighting' headdress but wore a 'staff' cocked hat. As part of the Ordnance they wore plain white feathers in the hat. The full dress scarlet coat dates from 1839 and has blue patches on the collar. The blue cuffs had red flaps with an extra set of loops and buttons. The collar has a rectangular gold loop and the pocket slashes have three gold loops. The gold epaulettes could have a single grenade and one was on each turn-back of the skirts. For undress clothing the long blue frock coat with metal shoulder-scales was similar to those worn in other units but the broad red stripes on the blue overalls was a special distinction as was the gold band on the undress cap. The simple blue coatee was worn for stable dress as Royal Engineer Officers frequently rode horse on duty.

Page 83

The 3rd (King's Own) Light Dragoons
at the Battle of Sobraon
Artist: Henry Martens • **Engraver**: John Harris
Published June 8, 1846

As the 3rd Light Dragoons were at the Battle of Sobraon February 10, 1846, this plate seems to have been issued very quickly. Actually Ackermann was publishing separately a series on engagements of the 3rd King's and almost any print of the 3rd Light Dragoons in action might be suitable. The 3rd had been in India for the Afghan War wearing scarlet but around March 1842 had changed to blue with scarlet facings, still double-breasted. The Albert shako was approved in 1844 and although it was worn with a white cover, this only appears in later plates. So the complete plate could have been for a full dress occasion instead of a sanguinary battle picture. The embroidery on the rounded saddle cloth is of the White Horse of Hanover.

Page 84

Royal Foot Artillery
Officer Dress and Undress
Artist: Henry Martens • **Engraver**: John Harris
Published September 1, 1846

The Royal Artillery served everywhere, hence the UBIQUE' of their motto, but they were part of the Board of Ordnance, not the Regular Army of Cavalry and Infantry. The Board which included Engineering Ordnance and other services was broken up after the Crimean War, allowing the Royal Artillery to appear in the normal Army Lists. The Foot Artillery followed the infantry uniform whereas the Horse Artillery followed cavalry dress as they had to serve with them.

The 78th Highlanders (Rosshire Buffs)
Officer in Review Order
Artist: Henry Martens • **Engraver**: John Harris
Published October 1846

The Ross-shire Buffs were formed in 1793 and obviously had buff facings which they continued to modern times. The feather bonnet has dicing of red and white only, which appears to be an error. However in early days the central square was buff as late as 1842, then green. The officer's sporran has gold bells and tassels, which are black for the men. The regiment had worn since 1793 a Mackenzie tartan which was based on the Government tartan with the addition of two white stripes and one red, making a variation of Seaforth, which has been called the Ross-shire Military tartan. Obviously buff coloured facings were the distinction of the 78th and a further distinction came in 1807 when at Assaye they were awarded the Badge of an 'Elephant with Howdah' worn on the belt-plates and elsewhere. In 1881 they became the 2nd Battalion of the Seaforth Highlanders.

1st The King's Dragoon Guards
Officer
Artist: Henry Martens • **Engraver**: John Harris
Published October 21, 1846

Two plates of Dragoon Guards (the 4th and 6th) had already been published and described in this series so this third plate on the King's Dragoon Guards was not able to show any special new features. This senior regiment of Dragoon Guard had originally been a Regiment of Horse but converted to Dragoon Guards in 1746. The helmet with its flowing black plume had been introduced in 1842 and was due to be replaced in 1847. The single-breasted coatee had been worn since 1820 for Dragoon Guards and Dragoons, and was red with dark blue velvet facings, although the latter are hidden in the print by the gold lace on the collar, and the cuffs by the large white gauntlets. When the new helmet was introduced in 1847, this plate was altered and given a second state in which all were of the German pattern. An opportunity was taken to eliminate the dark blue saddle cloth, leaving the red edged black sheepskin.

60th (The King's Royal Rifle Corps)
Artist: Henry Martens • **Engraver**: John Harris
Published October 21, 1846

Originally a red coated regiment, the 60th gradually changed their uniform to dark green with red distinctions, influenced by the hussar style. The officers, who were proud of their expertise with rifles, adopted uniforms evolved from the jäger or huntsman's dress. The cap or Albert shako newly introduced was of black beaver with a large Maltese Cross plate in front and a black silk ball tuft, as seen on the officer in full dress. The rifle green dress jacket is single-breasted with black braid and three rows of buttons. The pelisse, following the precedent of hussars who wore a pelisse instead of an overcoat, was somewhat similar but unlined, with black fur as worn by the officer on the left. The sword was like that of an infantry officer but with a steel hilt carrying a design of crown and bugle. The leather equipment was black as were the officers' gloves.

60th The King's Royal Rifle Corps
Winter Dress, Canada
Artist: Henry Martens • **Engraver**: John Harris
Published November 12, 1846

When this Corps were serving in Canada in the 19th century modifications were made to the uniform for cold weather use. There are unusual features occurring only in this country. The Army reluctantly made concessions regarding overcoats and footwear but there were also private funds to provide underclothing for the rank and file in the Canadian winter. Shakos and undress caps often had the addition of local fur in varying styles, especially for officers. The 60th Foot was long used to freezing conditions and had varying headdresses, but the long footwear or 'beef-boots' were not only popular but necessary. Sealskin gloves may be seen on the officers who also had fur collars on their coats. These winter fashions depended on the officers commanding, but most officers chose from what furs were available. In India the Rifle Corps saw action in 1852.

The 11th Hussars (Prince Albert's Own)
Officer Full Dress
Artist: Henry Martens • **Engraver**: John Harris
Published January 12, 1847

The 11th Light Dragoons had been without distinctive title until Prince Albert became Colonel of the Regiment and they were converted to Hussars in 1849. The Prince Regent (i.e. the Prince Consort) brought them special distinction, and crimson became their special colour, as seen on the fly or bag of the busby, instead of the usual red. The jacket was all blue as for other hussars but the trousers of the 11th were crimson as the Dress Regulation for Officers states. Light Dragoons had blue shabraques but regimental regiments of Hussars were allowed a variety of colours: the 7th and 8th had blue cloth, the 10th and 15th had scarlet, but the new 11th had crimson as well as black sheepskin. It will be seen that even the officer's horse has a most distinctive crimson throat plume. The mounted band was very colourful, for apart from the crimson busby bags, the trousers and the shabraque, they had an all-crimson plume (instead of white over crimson) in their all-white fur busbies.

Page 90
The Honourable Artillery Company
Officer and Private
Artist: Henry Martens • **Engraver:** John Lynch
Published August 10, 1848

Strictly speaking the Honourable Artillery Company is not part of the regular army but an ancient armed body going back to 1537 in Armoury House, London, long before the Standing Army was created. It will be seen that the uniforms are similar to those worn by the Grenadier Guards with white ball tuft, but instead of gold lace, the Company cypher has silver lace, embroidery and buttons. The grenade on the shako plate and the officer's collar is gilt because it is on a silver ground (this reversal was also carried out in the Grenadier Guards' uniform). It will be seen that the summer white trousers are worn although three officers in blue undress have the dark trousers with red piping. There was also an artillery section to the H.A.C. They wore a blue uniform based on the Royal Artillery's but are not included in this Costume series.

Page 91
Cape Mounted Rifles
Officer
Artist: Henry Martens • **Engraver:** John Harris
Published February 1, 1849

In the early nineteenth century there had been mounted riflemen in Cape Colony, South Africa but it was not until 1828 that they were paid for by the War Office and then accepted as the Cape Mounted Rifles. The officers were commissioned and appeared in the Army Lists and their rifle uniform was covered in the Dress Regulations for Officers of the Army. Being riflemen they were dressed as a Rifle Corps but with allowance made for being in a warm climate. The basic uniform was dark green with dark green facings on collar and cuffs. Their black beaver cap was slightly larger than a rifleman's shako and had a drooping plume of black hair. The officers' swords were of the pattern carried by Light Dragoons and the equipment was black leather with silver ornaments. These mounted riflemen did see action, in particular at the Bettie of Gwanga in 1846 when they fought side by side with British heavy cavalry against the Kaffirs. Captain (later Major) George Jackson Carey of this corps worked with Henry Martens on prints for the Cape Mounted Rifles

Page 92
H.M. IX Regt. entering Allahabad
after the Wars
Artist: Henry Martens, from a sketch by B.D. Grant, Esq.
Published March 15, 1849

The 9th (The East Norfolk) Regiment of Foot had been serving in the Sutlej Campaign from December 1845 to February 1846 and received three battle honours in June 1847, to be added to the tattered regimental flags (issued in 1827 and replaced in 1848). At first glance, the uniforms of the 9th Foot look similar to those of any other infantry of the line with yellow facings. Even the headdress covered with white material hid the regimental shako plates or badges which might be 'IX' or 'Britannia.' The latter had been the Norfolk's special badge since the beginning of the century – the seated figure of Britannia with lance in the right hand and the spear (or trident) in the left hand. It is the regimental colours that identify, from a sketch made by Lieutenant Bethune Donald Grant of the 35th Bengal Native Infantry who had seen the entry of the 9th into Allahabad.

Page 93
1st Life Guards
Corporal
Artist: Alfred de Dreux • **Engraver:** John Harris
Published July 10, 1849

Messrs. Ackermann had published a plate of an officer of the 1st Life Guards in May 1842 in which only the back of the other ranks appeared. Rarely do changes appear in the dress of the Household Cavalry but now a front view of a Corporal is shown. He has the red flask-cord of the 1st Life Guards and the white sheepskin with a broad edge of blue cloth. His rank in indicated by the gold chevrons on his upper right arm. In the early days of regiments of horse the senior non-commissioned officer was a corporal who was equal in rank to a sergeant of infantry even though he only had two chevrons. Later there was created a corporal of horse, a higher rank, which did have three chevrons, and later still, when aiguillettes of rank were introduced, they were worn by corporals of horse but not by plain corporals. But later, to distinguish non-commissioned officers in the Household Cavalry, a crown was added above the chevrons to mark the connection with Royalty and not as a rank change.

Page 94
The Royal Marines
Field Officer, 2nd Lieutenant
Artist: Henry I. Daubrawa • **Engraver:** John Harris
Published April 20, 1850

In the early days of the British Army, it was usual for regular soldiers to be on ship to maintain discipline. Then in the 18th century marines were found on the ships. They were then formed in divisions stationed at Plymouth, Portsmouth, Chatham and Woolwich. Thus the Marine colours, like that held by the 2nd Lieutenant (Ensign), were not allocated to regiments but to Divisions. In the 18th century the Marines wore an infantry red coat with white facings, later with Royal blue facings and gold lace and buttons. Officers wore epaulettes and as frequent inspections were held, a senior officer needed a horse as shown in the plate – and may have been called a 'Horse Marine.' Marines were made Royal after 1802, thus gaining blue facings, and the drummers the red coat as worn in Royal infantry regiments, but with their own pattern of white lace with a blue 'turtle' design.

Page 142
Madras Horse Artillery
Officers in Full Dress
'D' Troop
Published September 22, 1843

The Madras Artillery was a large corps with the Horse Artillery stationed at Bangalore, and with four batteries of the Foot Artillery, the first at Seconderabad, the 2nd and 4th at Mount and the 3rd at Kampree. The officers of the Horse Artillery were permitted to carry on their appointments the battle honours of Java, Mahidpoor and Nagpore. The corps had been formed in April 1805 from the Foot Artillery as well as the Native Cavalry. A Rocket Troop was formed in December 1806. The troops were lettered A, B, C and D for the European troops, with E and F for the Native Horse Artillery. After the Mutiny the four white troops became A, B, C and D troops of the 3rd Royal Artillery Brigade. Once again Captain Ainslie helped to provide information to Martens. The 'Roman' helmet had a scarlet hair mane and an elaborate gilt plate. The blue jacket had scarlet collar and cuffs with much gold braid and embroidery for the officers. Light blue overalls in early sketches were changed to strong blue later.

Page 143
Nizam's Army
3rd Cavalry (British) Army in Full Dress
Published September 20, 1845

The Army of Hyderabad was raised by the Nizam and offered to the British for service. The original rissaldars of the Nizam's Horse were converted into regiments in 1816. By 1826 there were five regiments of Nizam's Cavalry in which the present cavalry was numbered the 3rd. The title of 'Nizam's Army' was discontinued in 1854 when it became the Hyderabad Contingent. In 1890 the cavalry were named Lancers. In 1903 all entered the new Indian Army and the 3rd disappeared. In the plate the 'Roman' helmet with the red hair plume appears again and the gilt plate in front carries regimental distinctions. The dark green jacket and overalls appear almost black, which is the colour of the belts. However the mass of gold cord, lace and embroidery sets a high standard which is repeated in the style of the saddle cloth of a mounted officer in full dress. In the corner appears the gold crescent over the interlinked letters NCO. The horse's red throat plume also has a small gilt crescent, useful for attaching a picketing rope.

Page 144
Nizam's Army
(3rd Cavalry) Native Officer in Full Dress
Published September 29, 1845

When the three regiments of the Nizam's Horse were formed in 1816 they had been commanded by native chiefs but these retired in 1825. This left more junior native officers in direct control of the fighting sowars, although European officers held the higher commissions. Once again Captain Ainslie provided the information for the Nizam's Third Cavalry, although there is no information for this plate in his album. As may be expected the native officer also has the dark green and gold embroidery for his alkalak. The black leather belt over the left shoulder has gilt chains and pickers, thus indicating the use of a revolver. The gold and red twisted turban has a section which went under the chin to keep the turban in place, a distinctive characteristic of the Hyderabad Cavalry. He wears loose white breeches or pyjamas with the high black 'Napoleon' boots, as still worn by the Household Cavalry. The print clearly shows the bridle as red and black with heavy red fabric tassels. The red saddle cloth has a broad green border and wide blue fringes.

Page 145
Nizam's Army
Foot Artillery, Native Officer and Gunner
3rd Infantry, Native Officers and Sepoy
Published October 17, 1845

The four assorted figures have been supplied by Captain Ainslie to include the Foot Artillery and the infantry formed by the Nizam. A preliminary water colour covers the four types but the infantry officer who was on the extreme left has now moved to a central position. The number of infantry battalions had increased to eight by this time and although disbanded and reformed, there were sufficient Hyderabad Infantry to form the Hyderabad Regiment in 1903. The infantry officer with his scarlet coatee and gilt wings could pass for a European Officer except for the stout blue and gold turban. Similar comment could be made for the sepoys. The officer of the Foot Artillery has the blue coatee with scarlet facings and gold lace and buttons, copying the Royal Artillery. But his elaborate turban has gold cords with blue tassels on the right, differing from the infantry officer who has his on the left.

Page 146
Nizam's Army
(3rd Cavalry Sowar or Trooper)
in Full Dress
Published November 1845

Originally Captain Ainslie provided Henry Martens with information on the 3rd Nizam's Cavalry – three of the colourful sowars wearing the traditional green cord and alkalak which fastens on the right side. No sign of gold on the practical garments. Even the turban folds under the chin are broader and look firm. The arms of these cavalry men are the sword and the lance. One feels that the sword was the fighting weapon. The lance could be a fearsome weapon if the lancer was well trained but at the moment the lance is popular with the broad red and green pennant. This colour combination is repeated on the native saddle cloth. The horse harness appears to be in red leather but none of the officer's fancy tassels appear here. The harness is shown in a preliminary water-colour by

Henry Martens (in the Ainslie Album) which is made from a view point not followed in the final plate. Possibly the harness is in the softer red morocco leather.

Page 147
Madras Infantry (32nd Regiment)
Havildar, Sergeant, Sepoys, Private and Orderly Boy
Artist: Henry Martens (after Captain Frederic Ainslie)
Published November 12, 1845

The Madras Infantry regiments could number up to 52 and each was strong with its own distinctions. The facings of the 32nd were pale yellow and had the honour for 'AVA.' On the extreme left the Orderly Boy wears a white double-breasted jacket with yellow collar and cuffs, and elaborate wings of red and white with dark green fringes. His red arm band has three white chevrons which gives him temporary rank. Next to him is the subedar with his true rank of sergeant as well as the crimson sash around his waist with the tassel ends hanging on the left. His sword belt carries a yellow metal whistle and chain. His dark turban has an elegant badge of red and white. The two sepoys represent a flank company and a battalion company, as shown by their differing wings and shoulder straps, the former being in parade dress and the latter ready for active service.

Page 148
H H The Nizam's Cavalry
(3rd Regiment) Officers in Undress
Artist: Henry Martens (after Captain Frederic Ainslie)
Published January 15, 1846

Once again Captain Ainslie supplies information on a different uniform for the 3rd Cavalry, officers undress in dark green with white collar and cuffs, and gold lace and embroidery. The undress cap has a gold lace band and the piping of a lancer regiment. The black leather belt and pouch have gilt fittings. There are gilt shoulder pieces which could indicate rank, and the officer wears short white gloves and steel spurs. The iron scabbard of the sword indicates slings on the black waist belt. The undress overalls have double stripes of white cloth down the outside. The leather pistol holsters have no special colours and the rounded green horse cloth or shabraque has only a simple white line. The tan leather harness is lightened by a scarlet hair throat plume.

Page 149
Madras Cavalry and Horse Artillery
Officers in Undress
Published January 20, 1846

The full dress of the Madras Cavalry and the Horse Artillery has been covered already in Plate 3 and Plate 5, so Captain Ainslie now supplies the undress versions. The Light Cavalry jackets of French grey had facings of pale yellow, orange, buff or deep yellow, colours also worn on the side seams of the overalls. On the jackets, officers had silver lace and buttons as well as silver shoulder scales. In the plates, only the plain backs of the sabretache may be seen and these may be the black patent leather pattern worn for undress. The officer on the left wears the frock coat of stylish cut and dark blue colour worn by many officers without any notable distinction, even in the black braid on the front. On the right an Artillery officer follows the British fashion – blue, scarlet and gold. Perhaps the gold embroidered grenade on the cap is the only distinction, although the gilt shoulder scales may carry an indiscernible device. The native cavalry men in the background include a native officer with a plain black sabretache.

Page 150
Bombay Horse Artillery
Officer's Full Dress
Published February 18, 1846

The Bombay Presidency had both Horse and Foot Artillery with many honours, the former being based in Poona and the latter in Ahmednuggar and Bombay, while there was a Golundauze Battery also in Ahmednuggar. As may be expected, jackets were blue cloth, scarlet facings and gold lace. The Horse Artillery use the same pattern garment as the Royal Horse Artillery with five rows of domed buttons, the design of which was three cannons inside a circle bearing the words 'Bombay Artillery.' Officers had a feature not covered by the regulations: the end of the loops on the left, instead of fastening over the central row of buttons, were threaded through one another in chain fashion. Thus the garment was soon removed by hook and eye. The 'Roman' helmet was worn but in this Presidency with black hair plumes, not the striking red of other Presidencies. The 1st or Leslie's troop had a special plate with the badge of an eagle. A turban of leopardskin was worn by this Brigade.

Page 151
The Governor's Body Guard
Madras Presidency
Published March 12, 1846

All three Presidencies had their own Body Guard and there was also another Body Guard for the Viceroy. They were not mentioned in the early army lists and registers. The officers wore uniform from existing regiments and were often temporary appointments. There was one common feature and that was the preference for a scarlet coat or body garment. The only Body Guard shown in the Indian series is the Madras, based on Captain Ainslie's information. The costume roughly follows that worn in the British Army. The broad-topped shako was as worn by light cavalry and hussars. Red shakos had been worn by British hussars and yeomanry. The scarlet jacket with its mass of silver lace and embroidery was distinctive and became an Indian tradition. The sabretache and shabraque were scarlet with silver lace and embroidery and a tigerskin was a special saddlecloth.

Page 152
The Governor's Body Guard
Madras Presidency
Published March 12, 1846

No official date has been found for the change from the red uniforms to the blue but it could have been soon after this plate was issued, and after Captain Ainslie had returned to India. There was no problem in producing the new uniforms, in fact the original engraved plate was utilised, only the colouring process changing. Unfortunately the date of the change is omitted, the early date being retained. The new uniform still followed the practices used in England, still keeping to silver lace as worn by military volunteers, and not the gold, the prerogative of the Regular Foot. The tigerskin is still retained and collar and cuffs are the basic jacket colour. Although the native guard have blue turbans, they later began wearing red turbans as in the original plate. Captain Ainslie gave Henry Martens the information on the red uniforms but when the actual uniform changed to blue, the original plate had to follow suit. Luckily the changes were only in the colours. The same engraved plate was used but now with the new colours. Unfortunately the date of the new state was not engraved in the plate and thus the original (but misleading) date continued.

Page 153
Bengal Infantry
65th Regiment, Marching Order
Published March 25, 1846

There were at least seventy-four regiments of infantry in the Bengal Army all wearing the red jacket or coatee with a wide variety of facings. The 65th Native Infantry had yellow facings and the additional title of 'Volunteers.' They did not mutiny and were among the twelve regiments which survived; later they were renumbered as the 10th Bengal. The native turban of earlier years had been replaced by a peakless shako. It could have been plain black but here it seems to have a waterproof cover. The sepoys are in marching order, an equipment in which they had to march miles to a new camp or station. With musket and bayonet they were armed for any conflict on the way, and although they are not carrying food one may see on the top of their packs that they have vessels for water. Although 'reversed' facings were obsolete in the British Army, the drummer reclining under the tree has a yellow jacket with red collar and cuffs. As musicians were often from a 'mixed marriage,' they were allowed to have peaks on their shakos in European fashion. The red shako with white plume was popular for native bands or drummers.

Page 154
Nizam's Army
Camel Gunner, 3rd Cavalry
Full Dress
Published April 18, 1846

Once again the Nizam's Army is shown by Captain Ainslie to have unusual features. A cavalry regiment would have horse for action but the Indians always had a few camels for domestic duties. But here the unlikely animals were forced into violent action by having small 'cannon' mounted on their backs. The dress of the 'gunners' is that of the 3rd's trooper or lancer and the camel has a red and green saddlecloth draped with many green cords. As a special extra there is a red and green cap for the camel. In the preliminary sketches, it seemed as though the cap covered the eyes of the camel, so that it would be unaware of what its rider was doing. The flintlock musket or zamburak (wasp) rested in a metal 'U' shaped support which could be swiveled in any direction. The gunner has his head swathed in the red turban, a device which even the camel might have appreciated.

Page 155
Bombay Lancers
Officer, Full Dress
Published April 23, 1846

The plate is only noted as 'drawn by Hy. Martens' so Captain Ainslie may have returned to India although his name appears later. Bombay Light Cavalry had begun this Indian series but now more specific information may have been gained. There were three regiments of light cavalry; by 1842 the 1st became Lancers and after the Mutiny, all three became Silladar Light Cavalry. The first plate of Bombay Cavalry shows the officer in the light blue-grey jacket called 'cavalry grey,' but this new plate shows a deeper blue, not confirmed by 1850 regulations which quote 'cavalry grey.' The facings were white for all three regiments with silver lace and buttons. The lance cap has a trencher top of scarlet cloth, a colour not reflected elsewhere in the uniform. Also the fittings and cords were gold, not silver, which shows how difficult Indian uniform could be. The sabretache of French grey and silver had a 'star-over-8LC' backed with crossed lances.

Page 156
Madras Infantry
Bandmaster and Musicians
Published November 1, 1846

Credit is given here to Captain F. Ainslie but there seem to have been problems with the colouring: perhaps the Captain had returned to India. Following the fashion of British bands wearing white coatees from 1833, Indian bands did likewise. Originally the collar and cuffs were in the regimental facing colour but it will be seen that the band sergeant and the band are wearing white with red collar, cuffs and turned-back skirt, instead of the yellow facing of the others. The officer on the right does wear the expected garment but it was not usual for an officer at that time to be in charge of a band. He has silver epaulettes and a red pom-pom, both suitable for a bandsman, but his sword is a fighting type and not the thin curved type usual for bandsmen. There is a second state of this plate where all the white coats are changed to red, but this does not make all clear. The bandsmen still retain their red collars, cuffs and skirts; the officer on the right now has a red coatee with yellow facings. His silver epaulettes are now gold as is his lace, looking exactly as a fighting officer's. The band sergeant now has an all-white shako – perhaps because colour has been forgotten.

Page 157
Bengal Foot Artillery
Officers, Full Dress and Undress
Published May 14, 1846

The Bengal Artillery had three Brigades of Horse Artillery and seven battalions of Foot Artillery. As usual the dress was based on that of the Royal Artillery but with minor variations. A Standing Order of 1845 introduced changes: the elaborate embroidery on the collar was changed to flat gold lace on the collar and flaps, as appears in this print. Trousers were to be made of blue cloth instead of grey, with a single broad red stripe down the side for foot artillery. The undress blue jacket which had plain scarlet cuffs and collar now has gilt shoulder scales and studs, added in 1841, as shown on the officer on the left. In full dress the sword was slung from a white leather shoulder belt but in undress it hung from a narrow waist belt.

Page 158
Bengal Horse Artillery
in Full Dress & Undress
Published May 25, 1846

This plate was 'Drawn by Henry Martens' with no mention of Captain Frederic Ainslie although this was a print in his album. Plates of the Horse Artillery of the other two Presidencies had been published. The Bengal Artillery Was 'ancient:' the first troop was formed in 1800 and in 1801 served in Egypt to gain the honour of the Sphinx, which appeared on the officers' appointment as seen in this plate. There had been three Brigades of Horse Artillery, the Head Quarters in Dum Dum, the 1st Brigade at Kumaul, the 2nd at Meerut and the 3rd at Cownpore. The officers' full dress was based on the Royal Horse Artillery's but always with the 'Roman' helmet, the leopardskin turban and the fine scarlet plume which brought them the nickname of the 'Red Men.' It will be seen that even the undress jacket had much gold lace and embroidery as seen on the second mounted officer. Although the officers' full dress had gold laced overalls, for active service the mounted gunners had white breeches and high 'Napoleon' boots.

Page 159
Bengal Infantry
Light Company, 65th Regiment
Full Dress
Published May 30, 1846

This is the last plate for which information was supplied by Captain Frederic Ainslie. Plate 15 was also on the 65th Regiment of Native Infantry but depicting the Marching Order. The red coatee with yellow facings marks the regiment, the wings with the white worsted edges indicate a flank company and the dark green ball-tuft on the shako is for light infantry. The black shako has braid around the top and a yellow badge in front, while the brass chin scales are not needed under the chin but fasten above the regimental badge. The white overalls make a contrast which enables the brush and picker to be seen. The black leather sandals or shoes have evolved into a satisfactory foot covering but the cut-out sections show bare flesh (and no socks).

Page 160
The 35th Bengal Light Infantry
Officers
Published June 24, 1846

From this plate onwards they are noted as 'Drawn by Henry Martens' with no mention of Captain Ainslie, although he may have left information behind. There were several light infantry regiments in the Bengal Army but they all assumed a similar uniform, differing by the regimental colour of the facing; white in this case, red or pea green for the others, but the dark green ball-tuft was worn by all. The back view of the dismounted officer shows how long the cords of the crimson light infantry sash hung. The false pocket flaps with gilt buttons were discontinued in the British Army in 1844, but apparently not so in Bengal. The mounted officer in his blue frock coat has his shoulder straps edged all round with gold lace and with a gilt metal crescent. There were few mounted officers in the infantry regiment but they had a saddle cloth of the regimental facing colour (in this case white) with a border of gold lace, and for this regiment, gold embroidery of a crown over '35.'

Page 161
The 28th Bengal Infantry
Havildar, Native Officer, Band
Published July 25, 1846

Again the Bengal Infantry is drawn upon to show different aspects of uniform. This regiment has dark green facings and thus has a simple green flag without any special features. No mark for Queen Victoria, or even the East India Company, and it would not have been presented in a Christian ceremony. But it does have a gold tassel and a pierced gilt finial, which contains a cross recalling St. George. Once again the green ball-tuft on the shako and the green tufts on the wings of the saluting sergeant confirm a light infantry company as do the officer's whistle and sash cords. The sergeant is carrying a red 'marker' flag with 'XXVIII,' which could be used for drills or as a camp limitation. The band wear the expected white coats with dark green collar, cuffs and turnbacks, also wearing the striking red trousers (not seen in England) and the unusual red-topped caps usually reserved for lancer regiments.

Page 162
The 19th Bombay Native Infantry
Havildar, European Officer, Private
Published August 1, 1846

Now the infantry of another Presidency is chosen. Bombay had twenty-six regiments of Native Infantry and here the facings for the 19th are deep yellow. The officer in the middle is from the grenadier company as his wings and white pom-poms indicate. The braid-topped shako has a silver Maltese cross on the gilt star plate, a pattern which was continued on the next style of shako when it was introduced. The native sergeant has a similar shako but of cheaper material and, following the Indian fashion, no peak. It was said that peaks were only for those of European descent. He wears the white ball-tuft and scarlet wings with white tape and worsted fringe. As a sergeant he is allowed to carry a shorter firearm and on his right hip may be seen a small black pouch for caps or ammunition. In the background are the drum-major and several drummers dressed in coats of reversed facings – yellow coat with red collar and cuffs but white turn-back. The actual drums have a yellow body with red hoops. This corps of drums wear red shakos with black hair plumes, not usual as a band distinction, but in India many variations occurred.

Page 163
Cadets
East India College
Addiscombe
Full Dress and Undress
Published December 10, 1846

In the eighteenth century there had been a pressing demand for officers to serve on the three Indian Presidencies. The Royal Military Academy at Woolwich supplied many artillery and engineer cadets but this did not meet the demands, so in 1809 a college was founded at Addiscombe in Surrey and, following the example set by the Woolwich Academy, cadets at the new college wear artillery dress – blue and red plus an Ordnance badge. The Cadet in full dress with the white plumed shako and gilt epaulettes would appear to be a sub-officer, the equivalent of an under-officer at Woolwich. The white metal plate on his shako is a star of ten points which carried the Arms of the East India Company, with a gun or cannon below. The cadet leaning on the wall, wearing a single epaulette on his right shoulder, is a sub-officer. The man on the left with only shoulder-cords is not a junior cadet but perhaps a corporal, because he carries a cane to assert his authority.

Page 164
Madras Infantry
European Regiment (Officer)
1st Fusiliers, 2nd Light Infantry
Published April 14, 1847

All three Presidencies had European Regiments. At this time Madras had two, the 1st being normal fusiliers. In 1839 a second battalion was raised and named Light Infantry. Later, in 1853, a third battalion was raised. The rank and file of the regiment were of European descent and these battalions continued in being throughout the Indian Mutiny and in 1861 they became British regiments. The 1st became the 1st Royal Madras Fusiliers and the 2nd, the 105th Madras Light Infantry. After the re-organisation of the British infantry in 1881 the 102nd became the 1st Battalion Royal Dublin Fusiliers, and the 105th, the 2nd Battalion of King's Own Yorkshire Light Infantry. Unfortunately, in 1922 all Irish regiments were disbanded and the 2nd Yorkshire Light Infantry suffered the same fate in 1948. It will be seen that the uniform was distinctly British, the facings being blue on the fusiliers and buff (almost white) for the Light Infantry. The Fusiliers had the white ball-tuft but the Dress Regulations of 1891 ordered a 'red silk ball-tuft,' so some prints show this. The green tuft remained the same for the Light Infantry.

Page 165
The 11th Bengal Light Cavalry
Published July 12, 1847

The Bengal Light Cavalry has already appeared in Plate 2 dated 1845 but there were now some changes in the uniform. A General Order from the Commander-in-Chief dated 8th February 1847 quoted alterations in the dress trousers of European Officers of Bengal Cavalry. The dress trousers were to be of French grey (instead of dark blue) and there was to be a black beaver shako. In November the head dress or cap was to be made up as the pattern in use by the 11th Regiment – this being a body of regimental form, nine inches deep with a scarlet fly (or bag) and plaited top etc. So this particular plate shows what the 11th Light Cavalry were wearing in 1847. It will be seen that this was a busby, also worn by the sowars. Normally fur headdresses did not stand up to the weather or insects of India, so one may wonder how long it continued in wear. However the horse furniture remained similar to that in the earlier plate, but the crimson on the scrolls has disappeared and the black sheepskin now has a scarlet scallop edging.

Page 166
2nd Grenadier Regt.
Bombay Native Infantry
Officers visiting a Guard on Line Duty
Published August 9, 1847

A Bombay Native Infantry plate has been illustrated earlier (24th August 1846). This plate takes the opportunity to depict a European officer in undress and a native officer. The first two Bombay regiments of native infantry were both named 'Grenadiers' and had white facings; the 2nd had the early honours of 'EGYPT.' The mounted officer should have been a 'Field Officer' (i.e. Major or above), or possibly an Adjutant (appointed to that post). The simple wings have no rank badge, only a grenade to signify the grenadier company. Undress caps were constantly changing in style and detail. Bombay officers in 1823 were allowed 'foraging' caps of blue cloth with a leather shade (peak). Later regiments with blue, green or black facings were to have a black cap with a red band. Others were to have a band of the facing colour. Here one would have expected a white band, not blue. In 1890 the band was to be black silk lace. This plate may have the latter but another (exemplar of it) plate is known to have a gold band as a field officer might wear. The European officer wears a short single-breasted fatigue jacket but the native officer has the long-tailed coatee with gold wings, whereas the remainder of the guard have white tufted wings.

Page 167
Bengal Presidency
Officer of the Bundlecund Legion
(in Review Order)
Published August 2, 1847

The district of Bundlekhand (or Bundlecund) was occupied by the British in 1803 and again in 1809 after local disturbances. However, the area remained unsettled until 1838 when the Honourable East India Company raised a legion of cavalry, artillery and infantry with its headquarters at Jhansi. In September 1847 the cavalry was brought on to the military establishment of the Bengal Army with other irregular cavalry and the infantry became the 34th Bengal Native Infantry – to replace the old 34th which had mutinied in 1844. Unfortunately this unit also mutinied in 1857 and was disbanded. The Bengal Light Cavalry was ordered to wear a black fur busby in 1843 – and that is shown on the plate. It was nine inches deep and had a scarlet fly or bag. The blue alkalak with heavy gold embroidery was typical for irregular cavalry. The white gauntlets were not unusual, but the loose red trousers were, perhaps inspired by the crimson of Prince Albert's 11th Hussars.

Page 168
VIth Irregular Cavalry (Bengal)
European officer
Published October 1, 1849

The number of Irregular Cavalry units in Bengal grew gradually after James Skinner's rissalahs were established in 1805, eventually numbering up to seventeen. This Cavalry unit was raised in 1838 to serve in the Oude Auxiliary Force and was called the Cavalry Regiment. In 1840 it became the 6th Irregular Cavalry in the Bengal Army where they were known as 'Musketoons' as they were armed with that weapon. The officer in the plate could be the Commander, Captain James Mackenzie. Besides his tremendous black beard, he usually wears a distinctive metal helmet said to have an honour conferred by the King of Prussia and as worn by the Prussian Guard, bearing a large gilt eagle on the front. The red alkalak has a blue collar and cuffs, with much gold lace and embroidery. He does not wear European overalls but white breeches and the tall black boots. Instead of a shabraque, his horse has the native charjama of red and yellow sections. His sabretache has the blue face of light cavalry with gold lace and embroidery showing 'VI' over a crescent and 'B.I.C.' The sowars have red alkalaks and blue trousers whilst carrying white and red pennants on their lances – no sign of a musketoon.

Page 169
IX Bengal Light Cavalry
European Officer, Sergeant-Major, Private
Undress
Artist: Henry Martens
(from sketches by Lt. Wyndham, 9th Light Cavalry)
Published September 8, 1848

The Bengal Light Cavalry had already appeared on two plates of this series but now the undress garments of officers are recorded. Charles Wyndham had joined the 9th Bengal Light Cavalry in August 1843. His must have been a temporary rank as he was not confirmed as a Lieutenant until October 1851. The 9th Light Cavalry had orange facings for the collar and cuffs as may be seen. Some plates have a deep colour which has been described as maroon (a shade of red) but officially orange was the colour. The officer and the senior non-commissioned officer have undress caps with quartering welts and the narrow black chin straps. The man in the orange-reddish jacket is not named but may be a trumpeter. The man in the middle who may be a sergeant-major has a crown over his three large chevrons and carries a cane or a switch. The mounted lance-naique has on his left arm a white chevron edged in orange, and what may be a badge of a stirrup about to mark him as a roughrider.

Page 170
The Madras Light Cavalry
(1st Regt.) New Dress
Officer
Published May 24, 1848

The Madras Light Cavalry had been in two previous plates but now appears in a change of uniform. In September 1846 all regiments of the Madras Light Cavalry were to have facings of light buff, so the facings of pale yellow, orange and deep yellow disappeared. The same General Order now quoted five rows of buttons on the 'cavalry grey' jacket. The broad-topped shako had now changed to the shape favoured by the Prince Consort and the red and white plumes were now all white. The two stripes on the overalls were now changed to a broad one and three-quarter inch silver lace. The girdle, which was not clear in the earlier plate, is now seen as crimson cord held in place by gilt barrels. The rounded horse-cloth was changed to the pattern with long pointed ends and a black lambskin gave place to the skin of a cheetah; and the horse sports a long white throat plume.

Page 171
Sinde Irregular Horse
Commanded by Major John Jacob
Published June 5, 1849

The Sinde/Scinde horse originated in the Kutch Levy which transferred in 1839 to become the Scinde Irregular Horse. Early in 1842 John Jacob, a Captain in the Bombay Artillery, became Comman-dant of the Scinde Irregular Horse (he also was the A.D.C. to the Governor-General). It is possible that the mounted officer might be Captain Jacob but there were many officers in the enlarged Scinde Horse. Here is another unusual helmet but no information is available for it. There are helmets carrying this name, the plate of which was silver as were the chin-scales. The plume shown here is black hair but later the 1st Scinde Horse had white and the 2nd, primrose yellow. The dark green jacket is heavily covered with silver cords, lace and embroidery. The hussar sash is dark green with silver barrels. The dark green overalls have narrow silver stripes down the legs. The sabretache and shabraque are also dark green with silver embroidery displaying the cursive letters 'S.I.H' for 'Scinde Irregular Horse.' The sowar at the rear has a red turban and dark green alkalak, with high black boots, and his charger, a red and green horse-cloth.

Queen Victoria Her Majesty
Reviewing the First Grenadier Regiment Foot Guards

The Prince Consort
Field Marshal H.R.H. Prince Albert KG KT KP etc. Colonel of the (Scots) Fusilier Guards

Major General H.R.H. the Duke of Cambridge K.G.
Commander of a Division of the Army in the East

The Duke of Wellington
Field Marshall His Grace the Duke of Wellington

3rd (King's Own) Light Dragoons

16th (Queen's) Lancers

8th King's Own Royal Irish Light Dragoons

British Cavalry
2nd Life Guards (Officer)

British Cavalry
2nd Life Guards

Royal Artillery

Rifle Brigade
(The Brigade in Battle)

Trumpeter, Royal Horse Guards Blue

Royal Horse Guards, Blue

Royal Horse Guards, Blue
Windsor Castle

Royal Horse Guards, Blue
(2nd State)

42nd Highlanders

2nd Royal North British Dragoons

4th Royal Irish Dragoon Guards
Field Officer of the Day

The Royal Horse Artillery

11th (or Prince Albert's Own) Hussars

Officer of the 15th (King's) Hussars

12th Royal Lancers

1st Life Guards

IXth (or Queen's Royal) Lancers

The Royal Horse Guards

Officer of the 7th (Queen's Own) Hussars

Officer of the Queen's Own Hussars

XIIIth Light Dragoons

6th Dragoon Guards (Carabiniers) Officer

Xth (The Prince of Wales' Own) Royal Regt of Lt Dragoons

49th (The Princess Charlotte of Wales') Regiment of Foot
Officers of the Flank Companies

XVIIth Light Dragoons (Lancers)

The 2nd or Coldstream Guards

Ensign of The 1st or Grenadier Guards

VIIIth (The King's Royal Irish) Light Dragoons Hussar Officer

The 3rd or Scots Fusilier Guards
Light Infantry Skirmishing

21st Royal North British Fusiliers
Officers in Full and Undress

The 4th (The Queen's Own) Light Dragoons

XVIth (The Queen's) L.D. Lancers

The 6th (Inniskilling) Dragoons

6th Inniskilling Dragoons

Royal Engineers

The 3rd (King's Own) Light Dragoons at the Battle of Sobraon

Royal Foot Artillery
Officer Dress and Undress

The 78th Highlanders (Rosshire Buffs)
Officer in Review Order

**1st The King's Dragoon Guards
Officer**

60th (The King's Royal Rifle Corps)

60th The King's Royal Rifle Corps
Winter Dress, Canada

The 11th Hussars (Prince Albert's Own)
Officer Full Dress

The Honourable Artillery Company
Officer and Private

Cape Mounted Rifles
Officer

H.M. IX Regt. entering Allahabad after the Wars

1st Life Guards
Corporal

The Royal Marines
Field Officer, 2nd Lieutenant

Lieutenant-General and Staff

The 14th Light Dragoons
Officer in Review Order

The 93rd Sutherland Highlanders

The Rifle Brigade
Skirmishing Order

The 7th Princess Royal's Dragoon Guards

2nd (The Queen's) Dragoon Guards
Officer (Review Order)

6th Dragoon Guards
(Carabiniers)

The 74th Highlanders

3rd Surrey Militia
Review Order

92nd Highlanders

1st Royal Dragoons

2nd Royal North British Dragoons or Scots Greys

71st Highland Light Infantry

38th (1st Staffordshire)

1st (The Royal) Regiment
Drill ground, Dover

The 88th (Connaught Rangers) at Chobham

The 72nd Highlanders
(Duke of Albany's Own)

ACKERMANN SMALL PRINTS

13th Light Dragoons

10th Prince of Wales's Hussars

16th Lancers

1st Life Guards

Royal Horse Artillery

2nd North British Dragoons (Scotch Greys)

2nd Life Guards

Royal Horse Guards - Blues

17th Lancers

4th Royal Irish Dragoon Guards

11th Prince Albert's Own Hussars

14th Light Dragoons

Royal Foot Artillery

Grenadier Guards

8th Hussars

50th Foot

3rd Light Dragoons

The Rifle Brigade

42nd Highlanders

72nd Highlanders

5th Dragoon Guards

Scots Fusilier Guards

Coldstream Guards

4th Light Dragoons

Royal Engineers

15th Hussars

9th Lancers

General Officer

12th Lancers

7th Hussars

1st Life Guards

1st King's Dragoon Guards

Ceylon Rifles

3rd East Kent Buffs

6th Inniskilling Dragoons

7th Dragoon Guards

74th Highlanders

Cape Mounted Rifles

1st Royal Dragoons

92nd Highlanders

93rd Highlanders

79th Highlanders

2nd Dragoon Guards (Queen's Bays)

6th Dragoon Guards (Carabiniers)

23rd or Royal Welch Fusiliers

Rifle Brigade

The 93rd Highlanders

The Grenadier Guards

79th Cameron Highlanders

33rd (1st Yorkshire West Riding)

Royal Artillery

7th Royal Fusiliers

1st Life Guards

Scots Fusilier Guards

The Turkish Contingent

42nd Highlanders

10th Royal Regiment of Lt. Dragoons

4th Queen's Own Light Dragoons

4th Royal Irish Dragoon Guards

ACKERMANN'S COSTUMES
OF THE INDIAN ARMY 1844-1849

Bombay Light Cavalry (Officer)

(7th) Bengal Light Cavalry (Officer)

Madras Light Cavalry
Officers in Review Order

Madras Infantry
Officers of the Rifles and Light Infantry in Full Dress

Madras Horse Artillery
Officers in Full Dress

Nizam's Army
3rd Cavalry (British) Army in Full Dress

Nizam's Army
(3rd Cavalry) Native Officer in Full Dress

Nizam's Army
Foot Artillery, Native Officer and Gunner

Nizam's Army
(3rd Cavalry Sowar or Trooper) in Full Dress

Madras Infantry (32nd Regiment)
Havildar, Sergeant, Sepoys, Private and Orderly Boy

**H H The Nizam's Cavalry
(3rd Regiment) Officers in Undress**

Madras Cavalry and Horse Artillery
Officers in Undress

Bombay Horse Artillery
Officer's Full Dress

The Governor's Body Guard
Madras Presidency

The Governor's Body Guard
Madras Presidency

Bengal Infantry
65th Regiment, Marching Order

Nizam's Army
Camel Gunner, 3rd Cavalry

Bombay Lancers
Officer, Full Dress

Madras Infantry
Bandmaster and Musicians

Bengal Foot Artillery
Officers, Full Dress and Undress

**Bengal Horse Artillery
in Full Dress & Undress**

Bengal Infantry
Light Company, 65th Regiment

The 35th Bengal Light Infantry
Officers

The 28th Bengal Infantry
Havildar, Native Officer, Band

The 19th Bombay Native Infantry
Havildar, European Officer, Private

Cadets
East India College

Madras Infantry
European Regiment (Officer)

The 11th Bengal Light Cavalry

2nd Grenadier Regt.
Bombay Native Infantry

Bengal Presidency
Officer of the Bundlecund Legion

VIth Irregular Cavalry (Bengal)
European officer

IX Bengal Light Cavalry
European Officer, Sergeant-Major, Private

**The Madras Light Cavalry
(1st Regt.) New Dress**

Sinde Irregular Horse
Commanded by Major John Jacob

APPENDICES

Appendix 1

The Firm of Ackermann

Rudolph Ackermann had been born in Saxony but came to England to earn a living as a designer of horse-drawn carriages, and thus established a business in London in 1783. He then began to sell books and prints, publishing his first book in 1790 when at ninety-six, The Strand, London. Then in 1796 he opened The Repository of Fine arts at 101, The Strand which expanded into a flourishing publishing works.

Prints had been produced from wood-blocks or metal plates which had been engraved but a new process was evolving, that of using limestone. In 1798 Aloys Senefelder had produced satisfactory results by lithography. At first this new technique was used for writing music but soon artists realized the potentialities of shading instead of a hard strong line. This Messrs. Ackermann soon adopted the best stones and processes, and employed artists and persons not only in England but from the Continent to work for them.

When Thomas Rowlandson began drawing plates of the London Volunteers, Ackermann took on the production and over the years 1798-1799 some eighty-eight plates had been completed and appeared in the book of prints names The Loyal Volunteers of London. Although no other long series of military uniforms appeared, there were occasional plates which came on the market like that of the Horse Guards Parade, 1809 after A. Page and T. Rowlandson. When the Napoleonic wars were over, Ackermann, in 1817 Messrs. Ackermann, produced J. Atkinson's *Incidents of British Bravery during the Late Campaign on the Continent*, which consisted of sixteen hand-coloured lithograph plates. The text of the wrappers stated that lithography had been introduced into Britain in 1801 and shows that the firm of Ackermann was keeping up with developments.

In 1826 Rudolph's eldest son, also named Rudolph, following his father, opened his shop, which was named the Eclipse Sporting Gallery, at 191 Regent Street in 1830. It must be pointed out that there was no competition between them and, when the father died in 1834, the original firm continued in being until 1952.

The time was approaching for Rudolph the son to begin his series of military uniforms but there was another asset to be taken into consideration. Several techniques had developed to printing on stone, one being the chalk method and another the mezzotint, bit it was in 1840 that lithographers discovered that if the ink was diluted and use as washes, the variations of watercolour could be achieved. Another change was for young Rudolph to alter the name of his gallery to 'the Eclipse sporting and Military.' Of course when his father died, he discontinued the term 'junior.'

The major print production by Rudolph Ackermann was slowing down. There were now hardly any new uniform plates, although there was a small number of later Victorian volunteers, who were not dressed in very interesting uniforms.

But Ackermann had produced much other material, such as the Funeral of the Duke of Wellington, several series on military incidents, battles and 'scraps.' But in 1860 there is little to note, except perhaps prints on the Royal Navy.

After Rudolph's death in 1868 the firm of Ackermann continued under his son Arthur and developed into a fine art gallery. This was situated in Bond Street specializing in oil paintings of all subjects, but finally business ceased in recent years.

Appendix 2

Artists, Engravers and Sources

When a person sees the magnificent quality of the plates produced by Rudolph Ackermann there is at once a feeling of enjoyment and satisfaction with all the work placed into the production. One does not question the small details of the uniforms as they always seem so perfect.

To achieve this standard one must see how a quality arose and how it was maintained. The firm of Ackermann had acquired a high quality over many years of experience, making sure to draw the material from the best sources and produce by the best technical expertise.

Being in London many uniforms there to be observed and to give the accurate information from the best military sources like Whitehall and the War Office. The firm of Ackermann was able to employ young artisans, some of whom had already made their mark in the artistic world, at the Royal academy and elsewhere, as they had come from the continent of Europe.

Now to look at the artists employed on these plates, we begin at least in alphabetical order.

Henry I. Daubrawa was an early employee in this military field but not very well known for experience in uniform. He is usually quoted as 'flourishing 1840-1848.' He is thought to have been born in Paris where he died in November 1861 and little more is known as to what he did in England so he may have departed soon after this series.

Alfred de Dreux (or Dedreux) was born in Paris c.1810 where he died in March 1860 but his other work was not often military and he is known to have painted animals.

William Heath said to have been born in 1795 (to 1840?) was both a painter and an engraver and lived in Chelsea. There were only two plates of his in the present series but he did much work for other publishers.

The man who did so many water-colours over a long period for Ackermann was **Henry Martens**, perhaps from a Belgian family. He lived in London and exhibited at the Royal Academy and elsewhere. In his early days he needed help from the engravers or engineers but later his draughtsman ship was of a high quality. Contemporary water-colours and his still existing note-book show how he studied detail and noted changes in clothing as well as improvement in drawing horses from life.

As has been mentioned before, the final stages of making a plate were dependent on the quality of the engraver or delineator on the litho stone. These were often fully qualified artists who had even exhibited at the Royal academy, but needed regular employment paid weekly instead of waiting for the occasional purchase from a passer-by.

O.A. Driscoll was one who engraved many plates and served many years for Messrs. Ackermann, completing and often improving the artist's drawing but unfortunately nothing may be quoted about his life.

John William Giles was one of those who had exhibited at the Royal Academy but engraved a few plated in 1841-1842 for Messrs Ackermann but nothing further to be noted.

Louis Haghe (1806-1885) was born in Tournay, Belgium. He became proficient in water-colour and a lithographer when he was seventeen years old. He came to England in 1823 and worked with William Day on twelve of the lithographs in the *Costumes of the British Army*. He also produced plates for Day and Son, later to continue contacts with Belgium but died in Brixton in 1885 aged 79 years.

John Harris (1811-1865) was a Londoner and worked for both father and son Ackermann. He lived near Charing Cross Road and this not far from either junior in Regent Street or Senior in the Strand.

John Lynch lacks information although he is said to have died in 1865 and his few plates did not always do justice to the work of Martens.

Having dealt with those who were actively concerned with the technical processes, thanks must be given to those who were known to have supplied documentation of dress and period. The complete sources can be quoted but there are certain names quoted in the printed upon which background details may be found.

There is little doubt that the presentation of uniform was intended to be as accurate as possible and not an artist's rendering of a gallant hero. Many of the uniforms seen on the plates could be observed in London where advice would be given from authoritative sources.

But when it came to produce exotic uniforms of another continent such as India, the best way seemed to be to find someone who had seen and noted them. Such a man was Captain Frederic Ainslie of the 21st North British Fusiliers (later known as the Royal Scots Fusiliers).

Frederic Ainslie had been a second lieutenant in the 21st regiment of Fusiliers on April 24, 1825, then lieutenant on October 5, 1832, and eventually captain on June 26, 1838. He appears to have made contact with Messrs Ackermann when on lave in London about 1845. He then met Henry Martens and together they worked out details for many of the Indian plates before the officer returned to service in India, perhaps late 1846. In October 1848 he was promoted to major in his own regiment and then lieutenant-colonel in April 1852. The Fusiliers then left India and spent some time in Ireland. When the Crimean War broke out the regiment went into action and the good Frederic Ainslie was killed in the battle of Inkermann on November 5, 1856.

His brother Henry Francis Ainslie was a colonel in the 83rd Foot and on the death of Frederic an album which had been complied during his dealings with Messrs Ackermann contained sketches by himself and by Henry Martens for the completed plates which were also bound into the album. Inside the front cover is a photograph of two goblets which Henry relates that Frederic had made because 'he was paid for his assistance and bought two goblets with the money.' This unique album was eventually bought by Anne S.K. Brown in 1962 and is now in the collection at Providence as a most valuable record to see how the prints were evolved and printed.

Captain Frederic Ainslie seems to have collected all the prints for which he made sketches and gave advice to martens, finally printing when all was agreed. This his sketches, those trials by Martens and the final prints were bound in a fine leather-covered book, 15" by 11". They appear in no particular order and Ainslie began the album with a plate of his own regiment, which had appeared as Plate 27 in the *Costumes of the British Army*, published in February 1846 and showing full dress of the Royal North British Fusiliers. At the end of the Indian plates, he added several sketches which he had made of his own regiment but which were never published.

Another contemporary helper mentioned on a print was 'B.H. Grant Esq.' who made a sketch of 'H.M. IXth Reg. Entering Allahabad after the Wars.' This information was added to Plate No.46 in the *Costumes of the British Army*. This gentleman seems to be the Bethune Donald Grant (1827-1854) who was an ensign in the 35th Bengal Native Infantry at that time (he was made a lieutenant later, in May 1852). The 'Wars' referred to in that print were in the

Sutlej Campaign 1845-1846. Thanks are due to the Fine Art Department at the National Army Museum for the information on this officer.

As Captain Ainslie had disappeared, information on the Indian Army had to be sought from other sources and on Plate No.31 in the *Costume of the Indian Army* by Martens is written 'from a sketch by Lt. Wyndham of the 9th Bengal Light Cavalry.' Charles Wyndham (1827-1908) became a cornet in the East India Company service on May 22, 1843 (aged sixteen years) and became a lieutenant in the 9th Bengal Light Cavalry in 1851 but retired to England in 1855 (aged twenty-eight).

It would seem that the two plates on the Cape Mounted Rifles (No.40 of *Costume*, February 1849, and of the 'Small' series, November 1853, by Henry Martens) had advice from George Jackson Carey, who was a Captain from October 1848 and Major from January 28, 1853 in the Cape Mounted Rifles.

No other names are mentioned on the plates regarding sources of accuracy but there must have been many others who assisted in keeping the high quality of these fine colour plates.

Also from the Publisher

The Kaiser's Army In Color
**Uniforms of the Imperial German Army
as Illustrated by Carl Becker 1890-1910**
Charles Woolley

The author brings to the student of uniforms, as well as the art and military historian, the true glory of this brief, but most colorful time. The 104 never before published uniform plates are a treasure trove of color, action, and rarity which have only been viewed by a select few before this publication. The additional illustrations from books and the postcard art reproduced here well display the scope and depth of Becker's work.
Size: 9" x 12" • over 130 color plates • 152 pp.
ISBN: 0-7643-1173-5 • hard cover • $49.95

Historical Record of the 14th (King's) Hussars
1715-1900
Col. Henry Blackburne Hamilton

This reprint of the 14th (King's) Hussars unit history was first published in 1901 and appears here in a new quality edition. This complete history is presented chronologically and details the commanders, operations and uniforms from 1715-1900, and is complemented with superb full color plates of uniforms and standards, and duotone photographs of the regimental commanders during this period. Detailed maps show operational campaign details.
Size: 7" x 10" • 33 duotone photographs, 16 color uniform plates, 12 maps • 736 pp.
ISBN: 0-7643-0351-1 • hard cover • $59.95

TARTANS: *Abbotsford to Fraser*
William H. Johnston & Philip D. Smith, Jr.

In this first of three alphabetically arranged volumes you will find over 400 examples of vividly striped tartans covering the names Abbotsford to Fraser.
Size: 11" x 8 1/2" • over 400 color photos • 112 pp.
ISBN: 0-7643-0961-7 • soft cover • $24.95

TARTANS: *Frederickton to MacNeil*
William H. Johnston & Philip D. Smith, Jr.

Second of three alphabetically arranged volumes you will find over 400 examples of vividly striped tartans covering the names Frederickton to MacNeil.
Size: 11" x 8 1/2" • over 400 color photos • 112 pp.
ISBN: 0-7643-0962-5 • soft cover • $24.95

TARTANS: *MacNichol to Yukon*
William H. Johnston & Philip D. Smith, Jr.

Third of three alphabetically arranged volumes you will find over 400 examples of vividly striped tartans covering the names MacNichol to Yukon.
Size: 11" x 8 1/2" • 400 color photos • 112 pp.
ISBN: 0-7643-1029-1 • soft cover • $24.95

British Army Uniforms in Color
As Illustrated by John McNeill, Ernest Ibbetson, Edgar A. Holloway, and Harry Payne • c.1908-1919
Peter Harrington

Gale and Polden's postcards of British uniforms are now widely collected but little is known about the artists and few of their original paintings have survived. Now over 130 of these rare works are reproduced here for the first time in full colour with background information as to how the pictures were created. This book is a useful reference for postcard collectors, miniature modelers, as well as collectors and scholars of early twentieth century British uniforms.
Size: 9"x12" • over 130 color paintings • 144 pp.
ISBN: 0-7643-1302-9 • hard cover • $49.95

Head Dress of the British Lancers
1816 - to the Present
David JJ Rowe & W.Y. Carman

Here at last is a book dedicated to the head dress worn by the British Lancers Regiments, both regular, and volunteer, from 1816 to the present day. It is profusely illustrated with both color and black and white photographs of lance caps – the majority of which have never before been published – together with contemporary black and white photographs of officers and other ranks in full dress uniform, and reproductions of original color artwork. Each pattern of lance cap is fully described, including the materials used, with each component of the head dress specified for the officers, and other ranks, together with the method of assembly. The head dress includes the 1856 pattern lance cap as worn by the six regular regiments of lancers, a brief description of the various patterns of lance cap worn by many of these regiments prior to 1856, and a condensed history of each regiment, accompanied by an account of the full dress uniform worn by the officers of these regiments c. 1900. Additionally, there is a full description of the pattern of lance cap worn by the officers of the Bedfordshire, City of London, East Riding of Yorkshire, Lanarkshire, and Lincolnshire regiments of Yeomanry, and details relating to the head dress worn by six little-known corps/troops of volunteer 'lancers.'
Size: 9" x 12" • over 260 b/w and color photos • 272 pages
ISBN: 0-7643-1446-7 • hard cover • $75.00

Uniforms of Imperial & Soviet Russia in Color
As Illustrated by Herbert Knötel, dj • 1907-1946
Robert W. Kenny, Jr.

The images in this volume are from the Anne S.K. Brown Military Collection at Brown University, Providence, Rhode Island. The first one hundred images illustrate uniforms of the Russian Army from 1907-1920. Herbert Knötel's Berlin grouping consists of forty-five images done on the post-World War II scene, and includes those contracted for by the Military Intelligence Section, G-2, Berlin command in 1945. Officially known as "Series A," they were used to educate United States and Allied military personnel on the various elements of the Soviet Army. The final fifty images covers Russian/Soviet uniforms from 1921-1946.
Size: 9" x 12" • over 190 color paintingss • 200 pages
ISBN: 0-7643-1320-7 • hard cover • $49.95